## FRANCIS FRITH'S
# A TASTE OF THE NORTH-WEST

## THE FRANCIS FRITH COLLECTION

www.francisfrith.com

FRANCIS FRITH'S

# A Taste of the
# NORTH-WEST

REGIONAL RECIPES FROM CHESHIRE,
GREATER MANCHESTER, LANCASHIRE,
MERSEYSIDE AND THE WIRRAL

Illustrated with historical photographs from
The Francis Frith Collection

FRANCIS FRITH'S

# A Taste of the
# NORTH-WEST

Clitheroe, Friends 1894 34346x

Compiled by Julia Skinner

First published in the United Kingdom by
The Francis Frith Collection exclusively for Dorrigo in 2009.
Paperback Edition ISBN 978-1-84589-457-3

British Library Cataloguing in Publication Data

A Taste of The North-West
Julia Skinner

The Francis Frith Collection®
Frith's Barn, Teffont,
Salisbury, Wiltshire SP3 5QP
Tel: +44 (0) 1722 716 376
Email: info@francisfrith.co.uk
www.francisfrith.com

Printed and bound in England

Front Cover: **Rochdale, Church Steps 1913** 65603t
The colour-tinting in this image is for illustrative purposes only, and is not intended
to be historically accurate.

Every attempt has been made to contact copyright holders of illustrative material.
We will be happy to give full acknowledgement in future editions for any items not
credited. Any information should be directed to The Francis Frith Collection.

As with any historical database, the Francis Frith archive is constantly being
corrected and improved, and the publishers would welcome information on
omissions or inaccuracies.

# CONTENTS

Introduction    4

Snacks    6

Fish and Shellfish    14

Meat and Poultry    24

Cheese and Vegetable Dishes    40

Puddings and Desserts    48

Teatime and Baking    62

Index of Photographs    86

Index of Recipes    87

Free Mounted Print Voucher    89

# INTRODUCTION

*'Bless o' on us Lord wi' this gradely stuff*

*An' nudge me when ah've 'ad enough.'*

A Lancashire Grace, said before a meal.

Travel around the north-western counties of England through the pages of this book and discover a selection of the delicious traditional food of the area, as well as some of the stories and fascinating facts behind the recipes. Your journey will be given added savour by the historical images taken by photographers from The Francis Frith Collection, showing the people and places of Cheshire, Greater Manchester, Lancashire, Merseyside and the Wirral in the past.

Regional traditional dishes were developed from the local produce that was available to thrifty housewives who had to feed large, hungry families on a limited budget. Many of the old recipes also reflect the limited cookery techniques that were available in the past, as well as the skills of the cooks who were able to provide cheap and tasty meals with only a fire, a skillet and a cauldron to cook with, often producing the historical version of 'boil in the bag' meals.

This book is not intended to provide a comprehensive collection of the local recipes of the region, and some recipes are modern interpretations using some of the fine local produce that the area is famous for, but we hope that the food described within these pages, as well as the descriptions of traditional customs, local information and dialect words, will provide you with a taste of the north-west.

*'Grace before meals and grace afta …*

*Them that didn't get enough should'a etten fasta.'*

Blackpool, North Shore 1890  22886

# SNACKS

Preston, Church Street 1903  50069

# RECIPE

—·—

## Parched Peas

A local delicacy sold at Preston's markets is Parched Peas, served with vinegar or sometimes mint sauce.

For the most authentic results use dried maple peas if you can source them (in Preston they can be found in Booth's supermarkets), but otherwise use dried black-eyed peas. Wash the peas well, then put them in a bowl and cover them with boiling water (the bowl should be big enough for the peas to double in size), and leave them to soak overnight. Next day, rinse the peas well with fresh water, then put them in a large pan and cover them with cold water. Put the pan on heat and bring the water to the boil, then boil the peas hard for 10 minutes; reduce heat and simmer the peas for 1½-2 hours until they are tender, adding salt to your own preference in the last half an hour of cooking. Serve the peas hot in a bowl with a dash of vinegar and black pepper.

—·—

Lytham, The Pier and Donkeys 1914 67480

## Dialect words and phrases from the Blackpool area

**'Appen'** - maybe, perhaps.

**'Barmpot'** - a simpleton.

**'Bicker'** - to argue.

**'Champion'** - good, well.

**'Corporation pop'** - water.

**'Dule'** - the Devil (from 'th' owd lad').

**'Es getten a cob on'** - he is getting annoyed.

**'Jiggered'** - exhausted, or broken, not working.

**'Lugs'** - ears.

**'Moither'** - annoy, as in 'stop moitherin' me' - stop annoying me.

**'Nobbut'** - nothing but, merely, only.

**'Owt'** - anything.

**'Parky'** - cold.

**'Spittin' feathers'** - thirsty.

**'Tram stopper'** - a thick sandwich.

Blackpool, From North Pier 1906  53853

# RECIPE

—·—

## Pease Pudding

This recipe recalls the dried peas rescued from a shipwreck which once saved the people of Blackpool from starvation. The story goes back to the year 1799, when the Lancashire potato crop failed and the corn harvest was so poor that prices rocketed. On top of this, a freak storm broke along the coast, wrecking fishing boats, flooding inland and destroying or damaging many of the cottages. The people of Blackpool were now facing winter with little or no food reserves, and were unable to meet the prices being demanded inland, but the disaster brought its own answer to their problems. As the storm destroyed their homes and livelihoods, it also carried with it a merchant ship, sails torn away and rudder smashed. Despite their own suffering, men made their way down to the beach to try and help the crew of the stricken ship, which by now was aground and in danger of breaking up. Suddenly a giant wave lifted the vessel and brought it further up the beach, enabling the crew to be rescued before she broke up. Amid the debris were barrels, sacks and packages – it turned out that the ship's cargo was mainly provisions, the bulk of it dried peas. The people of Blackpool survived the winter of 1799-80 on a diet of peas, fish and cockles.

> 225g/8oz yellow split peas
> 1 chopped onion
> 25g/1oz butter
> 1 beaten egg
> Stock – bacon stock is best
> Salt and pepper

Soak the peas overnight, then rinse and drain. Put the peas and onion in a large saucepan with enough stock to cover. Simmer together with the saucepan lid on until the peas are quite soft, replenishing the stock if necessary. Allow the mixture to cool slightly, then put through a blender or liquidizer. Beat in the butter and egg, and test for seasoning. Pour the mixture into a greased pie dish, cover and cook for half an hour in a pre-heated oven, 170°C/325°F/Gas Mark 3.
Serve this dish hot with roast pork, ham or bacon. Cold leftovers can be fried in bacon dripping and served with breakfast bacon.

—·—

Blackpool, The South Jetty from the Wellington Hotel 1890  22881

Fleetwood, The Barrow Boat 1908 59940

Morecambe, Entrance, The Central Pier 1888 21080x

# RECIPE

—.—

## Potted Shrimps

Morecambe Bay is famous for particularly delicious brown shrimps, and potted shrimps are a favourite local delicacy.

225g/8oz unsalted butter
1 tablespoonful water
1 teaspoonful ground mace
2 good pinches cayenne pepper
Freshly grated nutmeg, a generous helping
450g/1 lb fresh shrimps (or 350g/ ¾ lb frozen shrimps or prawns, defrosted)
Salt

First of all, make clarified butter: melt the butter slowly in a small pan with the water, taking care not to let it brown. Pour the melted butter in to a bowl to cool, and place in the refrigerator and leave until the butter has hardened. Remove the solid butter (this is the clarified butter) and discard the liquid which has settled beneath it. Melt 115g/4oz of the clarified butter in a large saucepan with the spices, then add the shrimps or prawns, lower the heat right down and let them steep in the hot butter for 10 minutes – they must not cook in the heat or they will become tough. Taste for seasoning and add salt at this point, if needed. Pour the shrimps or prawns with the butter into small pots, and leave until the butter has set. Melt the remaining clarified butter and pour enough over the top of each pot to form a seal. Allow to cool, then keep in the refrigerator until needed. Take out of the refrigerator for about half an hour before serving, to allow the chill to go off, which gives the spiced butter more flavour. Serve with hot toast or crusty bread.

—.—

# FISH AND SHELLFISH

Southport, The Sands 1902  48588

# RECImPE

—.—

## Stuffed Mackerel with Gooseberry Sauce

Prior to Southport's development as a fashionable sea-bathing resort, the handful of people living in the area had earned their living from the sea. At the end of the 18th century there were thirteen trawl boats, catching a variety of fish dependent upon the season, but including sole, mackerel, skate, ray, herrings and cod, and the occasional turbot. Cockles and shrimp were taken daily, as were oysters when in season.

Gooseberries have long been a favourite accompaniment to mackerel in English cookery, and gooseberry jam also makes a delicious accompaniment to cold smoked mackerel fillets.

> 4 mackerel, gutted and de-scaled
> 1 tablespoonful chopped parsley
> 1 tablespoonful chopped thyme
> Half a teaspoonful grated lemon rind
> 1 tablespoonful lemon juice
> 25g/1oz soft white breadcrumbs
> Seasoned flour
> 225g/8oz gooseberries
> Sugar to taste

Pre-heat the oven to 180°C/350°F/Gas Mark 4.

Wash and dry the mackerel, and clean them. Mix the parsley, thyme, lemon rind, lemon juice and soft breadcrumbs and stuff the mackerel with this mixture. Roll the fish lightly in seasoned flour. Melt a little butter or oil in a baking pan and, when it is very hot, put in the mackerel. Put into the pre-heated oven and bake for 25 minutes, carefully turning the fish over halfway through.

Meanwhile, for the gooseberry sauce, simmer the gooseberries in very little water until they are soft. Rub them through a sieve and sweeten lightly. Warm the gooseberry sauce through before serving with the mackerel.

—.—

# RECIPE

—·—

## Herrings with Mustard Sauce

Fishing has always been important to the coastline of the north-west region. Flatfish (such as plaice and sole), hake, herring and mackerel are particularly popular. Herrings are highly nutritious and were a staple part of the diet in Victorian times. Here, the herrings are served with a savoury stuffing for a tasty lunch or supper. Mustard sauce is a traditional accompaniment to herrings in many parts of England.

4 large herrings
3 heaped tablespoonfuls fresh white breadcrumbs
1 heaped teaspoonful finely chopped parsley
A squeeze of lemon juice
Grated rind of half a lemon
Salt and black pepper
Oil for frying
25g/1oz butter

Mustard Sauce
40g/1½ oz butter
25g/1oz plain flour
450ml/ ¾ pint milk
Salt and black pepper
1 level tablespoonful dry mustard powder
1 tablespoonful wine vinegar
1 level teaspoonful caster sugar
Lemon wedges and fresh parsley sprigs for garnish

Remove the heads from the herrings, clean, gut and bone them. Wash the herrings and pat them thoroughly dry. Put the breadcrumbs, parsley, lemon juice and lemon rind in a basin; season lightly with salt and freshly ground black pepper. Melt the butter and stir into the breadcrumbs to bind the mixture, which should now be moist, but crumbly. Stuff the herrings with the breadcrumb mixture, and if necessary secure them with wooden cocktail sticks. Slash the skins crossways two or three times on each side; brush the herrings with oil and wrap each in foil. Put the herrings in a well-buttered deep baking dish; cover with lightly buttered greaseproof paper and bake in the centre of a pre-heated oven at 200°C/400°F/Gas Mark 6 for 35-40 minutes.

For the sauce, melt 25g/1oz of the butter in a pan; stir in the flour and cook for 1 minute. Gradually stir in the milk, beating well until the sauce is quite smooth. Bring to the boil and simmer for 2-3 minutes; season with salt and pepper. Blend the mustard powder with the vinegar and stir into the sauce; add the sugar. Check seasoning and stir in the remaining butter. Transfer the baked herrings to a hot serving dish and garnish with wedges of lemon and sprigs of parsley. Serve the mustard sauce separately.

Fleetwood, The Harbour 1894 33968

Chester, Eastgate Street 1923  73865

# RECIPE

—.—

## Salmon Baked in Pastry

Net fishing for salmon is one of the oldest industries in Chester. At one time there were sufficient salmon to support a community of netsmen, many of whom lived in Handbridge.

900g/2 lbs fillet of salmon
Salt and pepper
Lemon juice
1 tablespoonful olive oil
675g/1½ lbs puff pastry
225g/8oz onions or shallots
Half a teaspoonful chopped tarragon
115g/4oz button mushrooms
1 egg, beaten, for glazing the pastry

Pre-heat the oven to 190°C/375°F/Gas Mark 5.

Season the salmon with salt, pepper and lemon juice. Heat the olive oil in a large frying pan and lightly fry the salmon on both sides. Take the salmon out of the pan and leave to cool. Roll out the puff pastry on a floured surface to form an oblong shape large enough to enclose the salmon. Chop the onions or shallots very finely, and sweat them in the pan the fish was cooked in, together with the tarragon. Allow to cool, then spread over one half of the pastry. Thinly slice the mushrooms and place them on top of the onions. Season with salt and pepper. Place the salmon on top of the vegetables, fold over the other half of the pastry to enclose it all, and seal the edges. Place, folded side down, on a well-greased baking sheet and brush the top with beaten egg to glaze. Bake in the pre-heated oven for 1 hour, until the pastry is crisp and golden brown.

—.—

Parkgate, Loading Mussels 1939 P255011

New Brighton, The Tower and The Sands 1900 45163

# RECIPE

## Fresh Mussels with Parsley

The photograph opposite shows Wirral fishermen at Parkgate loading mussels into jute sacks ready for transportation to the restaurants of Cheshire and Liverpool. Shellfish are still gathered by some locals from the brackish sands to the north of Parkgate, but the commercial trade ceased in the 1950s.

    450g/1 lb fresh mussels
    15g/½ oz butter
    1 clove of garlic, crushed
    1 dessertspoonful chopped fresh parsley

Check the mussels and discard any that are open, as they are not safe to eat. Wash and scrub the remaining mussels. Pull off the beards, and use the back of an old knife to knock off any barnacles. Put the mussels in a large pan with the other ingredients. Put on the lid, and cook over a high heat, shaking the pan from time to time to ensure that nothing sticks and burns. Cook for only enough time to open the mussel shells, then shake again so that the liquid in the pan gets into the mussels. The whole cooking process should take about five minutes. Serve the mussels immediately in deep wide bowls with the cooking liquid poured over them, accompanied by crusty French bread to mop it up.

St Anne's, The Sands 1914 67490

# MEAT AND POULTRY

Blackburn, The Market and Town Hall 1894  34307

# RECIPE

—·—

## Cheshire Fidget Pie

The substantial dish of Cheshire Fidget Pie was often served as a supper dish to harvesters.

175g/6oz shortcrust pastry
450g/1 lb cooking apples, peeled, cored and sliced
225g/8oz peeled and sliced onions
350g/12oz bacon or gammon, chopped into pieces
Salt and pepper to taste
100ml/3-4fl oz stock, cider or water

Pre-heat the oven to 180°C/350°F/Gas Mark 4. Make layers in a pie dish of apple, onion and bacon or gammon until all is used, seasoning between layers with pepper and a very little salt. Pour over the stock, cider or water. Roll out the pastry on a floured surface and use it to cover the pie dish, trim the edges and use the trimmings to make leaf shapes to decorate the pie lid. Bake in the pre-heated oven for about 2 hours.

—·—

## Dialect words and phrases from Cheshire

**'Bullyed'** - tadpole.

**'Mither'** - to annoy or bother, thus 'stop mithering me' - stop annoying me.

**'Spence'** - the cupboard under the stairs.

**'Lommeryed'** - stupid, simple.

**'Me yed's all of a missock'** - My head's all in a whirl, I can't think straight.

Nether Alderley, Village Smithy 1896 37477a

## Local words and phrases from the Liverpool area

**'Ackers'** - money.

**'Jigger'** - a narrow passage between houses.

**'Delf'** - crockery.

**'Neshed'** - feeling very cold.

**'You're in Dicky's meadow'** - you're in real trouble.

**'Ollies'** - marbles.

**'Welt'** - a tea break.

**'Antwacky'** - old fashioned, out of date.

**'Jangle'** - a good gossip.

**'Woolyback'** - a non-Liverpudlian.

Liverpool, Dale Street 1887  20002

Liverpool, The London and North Western Railway Hotel 1890 26662

# RECIPE

—.—

## Scouse

The well-known nickname of 'Scouser' for anyone from Liverpool originates from a sort of stew popular in the Merseyside area known as Lobscouse, shortened to Scouse. The dish and its name were probably derived from a north German stew called Labskaus, which was popular with seafarers in the 18th and 19th centuries. There are many variations of Scouse, according to family tradition – one of them is given here, but is not claimed to be the definitive recipe!

225g/8oz stewing steak
225g/8oz breast of lamb
1 large onion, cut into large chunks
450g/1 lb carrots, cut into slices
2.25kg/5lb potatoes
2 stock cubes – preferably Oxo
2 teaspoonfuls vegetable oil
Worcestershire Sauce
Salt and pepper
Water

Cut the meat into large cubes and fry them in the vegetable oil until lightly browned all over. Transfer the meat to a large saucepan and add the onion chunks, then the sliced carrots. Peel and dice 450g/1 lb of the potatoes and place on top of the carrots. Half fill the saucepan with water, and add the crumbled stock cubes and salt and pepper to taste. Bring to the boil, then reduce heat and simmer gently for about two hours. Peel and roughly chop the remaining potatoes and add to the pan, with a few dashes of Worcestershire Sauce to taste. Simmer for a further two hours, then serve piping hot.

—.—

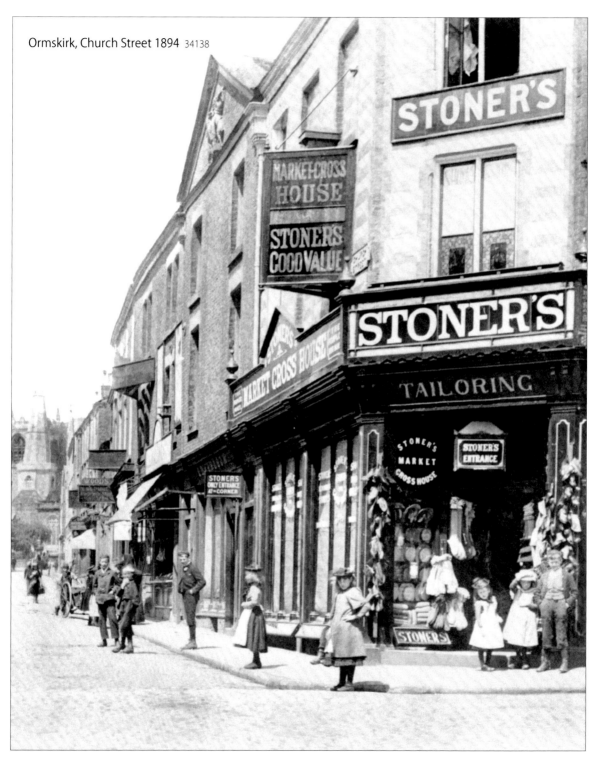

Ormskirk, Church Street 1894  34138

# RECIPE

—·—

## Beefsteak Pie with Lancashire Cheese Crust

Lancashire Cheese is the softest of the hard English cheeses. It has been made since the early 1900s and has a white, crumbly texture and buttery, slightly salty flavour that makes it ideal for cooking. Cheshire Cheese can also be used in this recipe.

For the filling:
1kg/2 lbs lean stewing steak,
   trimmed and cut into cubes about
   2cm (1 inch) square
2 tablespoonfuls seasoned flour
2 tablespoonfuls beef dripping or oil
2 onions, peeled and finely chopped
4 carrots, cut into thin slices
A pinch of mixed herbs
A pinch of ground nutmeg
Salt and freshly ground black pepper
600ml/1 pint beef stock

For the topping:
150g/5 oz plain flour
A pinch of salt
75g/3oz butter or margarine
75g/3oz Lancashire or Cheshire
   Cheese, grated

Pre-heat the oven to 190°C/375°F/Gas Mark 5.

Toss the meat in the seasoned flour until all the sides are coated. Reserve 2 teaspoonfuls of the seasoned flour. Heat the dripping or oil in a large frying pan and gently cook the onions and carrots until they are just softened, then remove the vegetables from the pan and place in a large ovenproof casserole dish. In the same fat, brown the meat cubes in batches, making sure that all sides are browned, then add the meat to the dish with the vegetables. Add the herbs and nutmeg to the juices left in the pan, and stir in the reserved two teaspoonfuls of flour. Mix well until all the fat is absorbed, then gradually add the stock, stirring all the time, until the sauce boils and thickens. Pour the thickened stock into the casserole, and mix it all together. Cover the casserole with its lid and cook in the pre-heated oven for about 1-1½ hours.

When the meat is cooked, make the topping: put the flour and salt into a mixing bowl and rub in the butter or margarine until the mixture resembles coarse breadcrumbs. Add the grated cheese and mix it all together well. Remove the casserole from the oven and sprinkle the topping evenly over the meat. Bake – uncovered – for a further 30-40 minutes, until the topping is cooked and golden.

—·—

# Bury Black Pudding

Black Puddings are a great favourite in Lancashire. They are made from pig's blood and oatmeal, cereal, seasonings, onion and flavourings. There are many local variations of black pudding recipes, but Bury is particularly famous for the version made and sold there – the herbs pennyroyal and thyme are believed to be some of the secret ingredients used in the Bury black pudding recipe. Black puddings are still sold in Bury's famous market, one of the largest markets in Lancashire, where they are served hot, with mustard.

Bury, The Market 1902  48562

# Local words and phrases from the Bury area

**'A bally ann meal'** - a meal put together from whatever was available.

**'Blather head'** or **'blether head'** - someone with a headful of nothing.

**'Blethering'**- chattering on about nothing.

**'Boggart'** - a ghost or spirit.

**'Chitty'** - a young girl or lass.

**'Chunner'** - to mutter.

**'Fettle'** - to repair or mend; 'to be in fine fettle' is to be in good shape.

**'Hippins'** - babies' nappies.

**'Keks'** - trousers.

**'Likely'** - handsome, good-looking.

**'Strap'** - credit, hence bought 'on the strap' is bought on credit.

**'Sennit'** - a week (seven nights).

Bury, Market Place 1895  36782

Accrington, Blackburn Road 1899  43496

# RECITE

— · —

## Lancashire Hotpot

Originally this dish of mutton, onions and potato was cooked in a pan over a fire. When ovens became more common in homes the ingredients were layered in a 'hot pot' – a tall earthenware pot – and then slowly baked in the oven. The hotpot lid was removed towards the end of the cooking time to brown the potato topping. In the days when they were cheap, a layer of oysters might also be placed beneath the potato crust. It is said that the dish was originally devised by cotton-mill workers' wives, who could prepare the dish in the morning and leave it to cook all day, to be ready to eat when the family returned from work. A woman's ability to make a good hotpot was said to considerably enhance her marriage prospects! As with many traditional recipes, there is no definitive recipe, but the dish is better the longer it is cooked – aim for at least 3 hours. Lancashire Hotpot is traditionally eaten accompanied by pickled red cabbage.

> 6 middle neck lamb chops
> 3 lambs' kidneys
> 225g/8oz onions, peeled and sliced
> 657g/1½ lbs potatoes, peeled and sliced
> Salt and pepper
> 300ml/ ½ pint lamb or vegetable stock
> 25g/1oz dripping or lard

Pre-heat the oven to 160°C/325°F/Gas Mark 3.

Trim any excess fat from the chops, and trim and slice the kidneys. Fry the chops and kidneys in a frying pan in their own fat for a few minutes, to brown them, then put the chops into an ovenproof casserole. Cover the chops with a layer of kidney, then a layer of sliced onions, then of sliced potatoes, seasoning each layer well with salt and pepper. Continue to place the ingredients in layers, seasoning each layer, finishing with a layer of potatoes. Pour on the stock. Melt the dripping or lard in a saucepan, then brush the melted fat over the top layer of potatoes. Cover the casserole with its lid and bake in the pre-heated oven for 2½ hours. Increase the oven temperature to 220°C/425°F/Gas Mark 7, remove the casserole lid and cook for a further 20-30 minutes to allow the potatoes to brown.

— · —

# The Cotton Famine

The other cotton-weaving towns of Lancashire suffered badly during the Cotton Famine of 1861-1865. This was caused by the blockade of the cotton-producing southern states of the USA by the north during the American Civil War, which prevented raw materials reaching Britain's cotton mills. Thousands of workers were made unemployed, experiencing great hardship, and Relief Committees were formed which ran soup kitchens and tried to find employment for some people on public works such as road-building. Rather than spend money on unemployment pay, most Lancashire corporations took to the idea of creating work for at least some of the unemployed mill workers to keep them from starving, and used their labour to create parks and public spaces. In Preston, Avenham Park, Moor Park and Miller Park were begun to provide work for some of the thousands of mill workers laid off at this time, and the residents of today still benefit from these green spaces around the city.

Preston, Moor Park Avenue 1903  50088

Styal, The Cotton Mill 1897  39616

## 'Welcome, Bonny Brid!'

The celebrated Lancashire dialect poet Samuel Laycock (1825–93) began work at the age of nine in a woollen mill in Marsden. In 1837 his family moved to live in Stalybridge, where he became a powerloom weaver. Between 1855 and 1867 Laycock wrote most of his best known poetry, including 'Bowton's Yard', 'Welcome, Bonny Brid!', and 'Lancashire Lyrics'. Laycock was laid off work during the Cotton Famine of 1861-1865, which prompted his twelve 'Lancashire Lyrics'; much of this work described in local dialect verse the conditions and disastrous effects that the widespread unemployment caused by the Cotton Famine had on areas heavily dependent upon the textile trades for their livelihood, and constitutes a valuable record of working peoples' experiences at the time. The first and last verses of 'Welcome, Bonny Brid!' are given here, which touchingly describe a father's love for his newborn child, despite his poverty:

*Tha 'rt welcome, little bonny brid,*
*But should n't ha' come just when tha did;*
*Toimes are bad.*
*We're short o' pobbies for eawr Joe,*
*But that, of course, tha did n't know,*
*Did ta, lad?*

*But though we 'n childer two or three,*
*We'll make a bit o' reawm for thee -*
*Bless thee, lad!*
*Tha 'rt th' prattiest brid we han i' th' nest;*
*Come, hutch up closer to mi breast -*
*Aw'm thi dad.*

# RECIPE

—·—

## Hindle Wakes

This recipe for cold, boiled chicken, stuffed with prunes and served with a lemon sauce, was traditionally served during the annual 'Wakes Week' when many towns and villages of Lancashire held local festivals and fairs, giving rise to its name of Hindle Wakes, or Hen-of-the-Wakes.

2kg/5 lbs boiling chicken
1 onion, peeled and cut into quarters
1 bouquet garni
600ml/1 pint chicken stock
For the stuffing:
115g/4oz dried prunes
175g/6oz fresh white breadcrumbs
¼ teaspoonful dried mixed herbs
25g/1oz grated suet
1 egg, beaten
Salt and pepper

For the lemon sauce:
25g/1oz butter
25g/1oz plain flour
450ml/ ¾ pint chicken stock (taken
   from the stock the chicken is cooked in)
1 tablespoonful lemon juice
To finish:
Finely grated lemon peel
Finely chopped fresh parsley

Soak the prunes in milkless cold tea overnight. The next day drain the prunes, chop them into very small pieces and combine them with the breadcrumbs, herbs, suet, beaten egg, salt and pepper. Stuff the chicken with the prune mixture, sew up the openings and truss the limbs. Put the stuffed chicken into a large saucepan with the sliced onion and bouquet garni, and cover with the stock. Bring to the boil, then reduce heat, cover the pan and simmer very gently for 2-3 hours until the chicken is tender. When cooked, lift out the chicken, drain and remove the skin and the trussing string before leaving it to cool on a serving dish. Strain the stock and reserve.

To make the sauce, melt the butter in a small saucepan, stir in the flour and cook for one minute. Gradually add 450ml/¾ pint of the strained stock that the chicken was cooked in, stirring all the time, until the sauce has boiled and thickened. Reduce the heat and add the lemon juice. Season to taste. Gently cook the sauce for a further one minute, then remove from heat and allow to cool slightly. Pour the lemon sauce over the cooked chicken so that it is coated and sprinkle with the grated lemon peel. Leave the chicken in a cool place for the sauce to set, and garnish with chopped fresh parsley before serving.

—·—

Lancaster, The Town Hall 1886 18091

# CHEESE AND VEGETABLE DISHES

Cheshire Cheese is said to be Britain's oldest cheese, and is mentioned in the Domesday Book of 1086. The crumbly, nutty Cheshire Cheese was originally made in Chester but is now made throughout the county; 'real' Cheshire Cheese acquires its flavour from the salt marshes of the region and was said to have been the favourite cheese of Queen Elizabeth I. Cheshire Cheese was described by the French in the following rhyme:

*'Into the Cheshire cheese, dry and pink,*
*The long teeth of the English sink'.*

The Cheshire Plain was historically a famous area for cheesemaking. For centuries, Cheshire Cheese was produced on nearly every farm in the region, and the matured cheeses would then have been brought to markets in the local towns, particularly to Nantwich, where an annual cheese fair was established in 1820. Production of this farm-made cheese peaked in 1907, when 600,000 hundredweight was produced locally, but the next year was to see the introduction of factory-processed cheese. Today there is only one farm left where the production of Cheshire cheese is totally bound to one farm, all the way from the breeding of the cows for the right milk to the maturing of the final cheese – and it is not even in Cheshire, but just over the border in Shropshire, although technically at least it is still in the Cheshire Plain region!

Runcorn, The Locks c1955  R67003

# RECIPE

~·~

## Cheshire Cheese Soup

600ml/1 pint good stock
275g/10oz peeled and diced potatoes
2 leeks, washed and trimmed
2 carrots, peeled and finely chopped or grated
25g/1oz oatmeal
115g/4oz grated Cheshire Cheese
Salt and pepper

Put the stock into a large pan, add the vegetables and seasoning and bring to the boil. Simmer for 15 minutes, then add the oatmeal and simmer for a further 10 minutes. Just before serving, add half the cheese and stir until melted, then pour the soup into serving bowls and sprinkle the remaining cheese on top.

~·~

Warrington, Church Street 1894  33805

# RECIPE

~ . ~

## Chester Potted Cheese

This is a good way of using up leftover pieces of cheese, as several varieties can be grated and mixed together in this recipe. It makes a tasty spread for toast.

> 225g/8oz grated cheese
> 50g/2oz butter
> ¼ teaspoonful ground mace or allspice
> 2 tablespoonfuls sweet sherry or Madeira wine
> Melted butter, to seal the surface

Mix the grated cheese with the softened butter and spice – adjust the amount of butter depending on how dry or moist the cheese is that is used. Beat well, then add the sherry or Madeira and mix well again. Put the mixture into small pots or ramekins, pressing it down well. Smooth the tops, then cover each pot with melted butter. The potted cheese should be stored in the fridge, and will keep well for several weeks as long as the seal is not broken.

~ . ~

Chester, The Cross 1903  49881

# RECIPE

—·—

## Cheshire Onion Pie

175g/6oz shortcrust pastry
50g/2oz butter
450g/1 lb peeled and sliced onions
25g/1oz plain flour
1 level teaspoonful salt
A good quantity of freshly ground black pepper
Freshly grated nutmeg
150ml/5fl oz single cream
1 large egg

Pre-heat the oven to 200°C/400°F/Gas Mark 6.

Roll out the pastry on a floured surface and use it to line a 20cm (7-8 inch) flan dish or tin. Line the base of the pie with greaseproof paper and fill with baking beans, and bake blind in the pre-heated oven for 10 minutes, then remove the paper and cook for a further 5 minutes to dry out the base. Melt the butter in a saucepan, add the onions and cook gently until soft, for about 15 minutes. Do not let them brown. Add the flour and stir in, then add the salt and pepper and freshly ground nutmeg. Gradually stir in the cream, bring to the boil and cook for 2 minutes, stirring, until thickened. Remove from the heat. Beat the egg lightly, spoon into it a little mixture from the pan and stir in, then add to the mixture in the pan and stir in. Taste for seasoning and adjust if necessary. Spoon the mixture into the flan case, level and grate a little more nutmeg on top. Bake in the pre-heated oven for about 45 minutes.

—·—

Macclesfield, Chestergate 1898 42600

# RECIPE

—·—

## Potato and Onion Cakes

Local tradition says that the Marshside area of Southport was the first place in England where potatoes were grown, after a ship was wrecked here in 1575 and its cargo of sugar and potatoes was washed up on the beach.

> 450g/1 lb potatoes
> 225g/8oz onions
> 50g/2oz butter
> Salt and pepper
> 150g/5oz plain flour
> Milk to mix
> Fat or oil for frying

Peel the potatoes and place in a saucepan of cold salted water. Bring to the boil, then reduce heat and simmer for 20-30 minutes until the potatoes are soft. Meanwhile, peel the onions, then either grate them or chop them into very small pieces. When the potatoes are cooked, drain and mash them and stir in the grated or chopped onion. Add the butter, salt and pepper and 115g (4 oz) of the flour, and mix it all well together to form a smooth consistency. Turn out the potato mixture on to a floured board and shape them with your hands into small flat rounds about 1.5cm (¾ inch) thick, and roll them in the remaining flour to coat them. Heat the fat or oil in the frying pan, and fry the potato cakes on both sides until they are golden brown. Serve hot for breakfast or high teas, with bacon, sausages or eggs.

—·—

Wallasey, May Cottage and the Nook 1898  W164012

# Wreckers and Smugglers

Though fishing was the principal industry of the village of Wallasey on the Wirral, James Stonehouse, who knew the area in the late 17th century, portrayed the inhabitants as a shifty lot who made their real livings through less legal means. He wrote that 'the inhabitants were nearly all wreckers and smugglers – they ostensibly carried on the trade and calling of fishermen, farm-labourers and small farmers; but they were deeply saturated with the sins of covetousness, and many a fierce fire has been lighted on the Wirral shore on stormy nights to lure the good ships on the Burbo or Hoyle Banks. There is scarcely a house in the north Wirral that could not provide a guest with a good stiff glass of brandy or Hollands.' Perhaps that explains why it was said that the flames had the blue haze of burning brandy on one of the occasions when St Hilary's Church in the village burnt down!

# PUDDINGS AND DESSERTS

Blackpool, Imperial Hydropathic Establishment 1890  22890

Southport, Lord Street 1913  66508

# RECIPE

~ . ~

## Summer Pudding

The hydropathic craze swept Britain from the 1840s onwards, when a German practitioner named Vincenz Priessnitz developed a series of health treatments using ordinary cold water, combined with dietary regimes, thus saving the need to visit a spa town. There were dozens of treatments on offer for the more affluent customers, including Turkish, Russian and American baths, electro-massage, Greville Hot-Air treatment, and Nauheim treatments for affectations of the heart.

Summer Pudding was a popular pudding with visitors to hydropathic establishments at towns such as Blackpool and Southport because it was lighter than pastry-based puddings, which were thought to be heavy and indigestible. For this reason it was sometimes known as Hydropathic Pudding.

> 10 slices of crustless white bread – use bread from a proper loaf, not a sliced and
>     wrapped one, for best results
> 3 tablespoonfuls of milk
> 750g/1½ lbs soft fruit – use a variety of (such fruits as) raspberries, cherries,
>     redcurrants, blackcurrants, white currants, loganberries or (sparingly) strawberries
> 115g/4oz caster sugar

Reserve a few pieces of fresh fruit to decorate. Lightly butter a pudding basin of 1 litre/1¾ pint capacity. Moisten the bread with milk. Hull, stone or top and tail the fruit as necessary. Cook it all very gently in the sugar for 4-5 minutes until the sugar melts and the juices run. Spoon off a few spoonfuls of the juice as it cools and reserve. Line the sides and bottom of the pudding basin with the bread slices, cutting them to fit where necessary and checking that there are no spaces. Reserve enough bread slices for a lid. Pour in the fruit, which should come almost to the top, and cover closely with the remaining bread. Put a small plate over the top (it should just fit inside the rim of the basin), and weight it with something heavy. Leave to press overnight in the fridge.

To serve, remove the weight and the plate. Place a deep serving dish over the top of the pudding basin and reverse quickly so that the pudding comes out easily in one piece. Pour the remaining juices slowly all over the pudding, especially over the places where the juice has not seeped through thoroughly. Keep cold.

~ . ~

# RECIPE

—·—

## Gooseberry and Elderflower Cream

Nine villages in central Cheshire compete every year at the end of July and early August in the old art of gooseberry showing. The gooseberries are weighed in the ancient measures of pennyweights and grains, and the growers compete in classes for the heaviest berry, twins, triplets and colours. The largest gooseberry ever grown was exhibited at the Marton Village Show in Congleton in 1993 – grown by Kelvin Archer, it was a Montrose Berry which weighed 39 pennyweights and 9 grains (61.9g - just over 2oz).

> 500g/1½ lbs gooseberries
> 30ml/2 tablespoonfuls elderflower cordial
> 300ml/10fl oz double cream
> 115g/4oz icing sugar

Place the gooseberries in a heavy saucepan, cover and cook over a low heat, shaking the pan occasionally until they are tender. Tip the gooseberries into a bowl, crush them with a heavy wooden spoon or potato masher, then leave them to cool completely. (The gooseberries can be sieved or puréed if a finer consistency is preferred.) Beat the cream until soft peaks form, then fold in half the crushed gooseberries. Sweeten with icing sugar to taste, and fold in the elderflower cordial. Sweeten the remaining gooseberries with icing sugar to taste. Put a layer of the cream mixture in four dessert dishes or tall glasses, and then a layer of crushed gooseberries, then cover and chill for at least one hour before serving.

—·—

# Bear Town

Congleton is sometimes known as 'Bear Town'. Bear-baiting was once so popular here that when the town's bear died just before the annual Wakes, the local people were so anxious to replace it so that the celebrations would not be spoiled that the Congleton Corporation used the money that had been set aside to buy a new Bible for the parish church to buy a new bear for 16 shillings (80p). The story is recalled in the bear that appears on the town crest.

Congleton, Lawton Street 1898  42154

# RECIPE

~ . ~

## Damson and Apple Tansy

Both Cheshire and Lancashire are famous for growing damsons. This old English recipe dates back to the 15th century, and took its name from the bitter-tasting herb of tansy which was used in the past for flavouring sweet dishes – however, 'tansy' is now used to describe a buttered fruit purée made with eggs and breadcrumbs, and the flavour is sharpened with lemon juice instead.

225/8oz damsons
225g/8oz cooking apples
50g/2oz unsalted butter
115g/4oz caster sugar
2 egg yolks, beaten
4 level dessertspoonfuls of fresh white breadcrumbs
150ml/ ¼ pint double cream
1 dessertspoonful of lemon juice

Wash the damsons. Peel and core the apples and cut them into thin slices. Melt the butter in a heavy-bottomed saucepan with 70ml (2½ fl oz) of cold water, cover the pan with its lid and boil the fruit over a low heat until it is soft, stirring from time to time to prevent sticking and burning. Remove the pan from the heat and either push the fruit though a coarse sieve or put it through a blender, to form a purée. Return the purée to the pan and stir in the sugar – add a little extra to taste if necessary. If the purée seems rather thin, cook it over a low heat until it has reduced down and thickened to a dropping consistency. Remove the pan from the heat and allow the purée to cool a little, then mix in the beaten egg and the breadcrumbs. Return the pan to a low heat and cook, stirring continually, until the mixture has thickened, then leave to cool.

Lightly whisk the cream and fold it into the cooled damson mixture. Add a little lemon juice to taste, to sharpen the flavour. Spoon the mixture into individual serving dishes or glasses and chill in the refrigerator for at least one hour before serving.

~ . ~

Altrincham, Old Houses 1903 49669x

# RECIPE

—.—

## Manchester Pudding

This recipe was included by Mrs Beeton in her famous 'Book of Household Management' in the 19th century. To make it particularly authentic, use damson jam.

175g/6oz shortcrust pastry
50g/2oz butter
25g/1oz caster sugar for the filling
Grated zest of one lemon
Jam – any flavour of choice
2 eggs, separated into yolks and whites
1 tablespoonful brandy
300ml/ ½ pint milk
50g/2oz fresh white breadcrumbs
115g/4oz caster sugar for the meringue

Pre-heat the oven to 190°C/375°F/Gas Mark 5.

Bring the milk to the boil with the lemon zest in the pan, and simmer for 5 minutes, to infuse the flavour. Pour the milk through a sieve over the breadcrumbs in a bowl. Leave to cool for five minutes, then beat the egg yolks into the breadcrumb mixture with the butter, sugar and brandy. Line a greased ovenproof pie dish with the pastry, and spread the base with jam. Cover with the breadcrumb mixture and bake in the pre-heated oven for 45 minutes – reduce the heat towards the end of the cooking time if necessary, if the top is browning too quickly.

When the pudding has cooked, make the meringue: whisk the egg whites until stiff, fold in half the caster sugar and whisk again until shiny. Fold in the remaining sugar with a large metal spoon, then spoon the meringue mixture over the pudding to cover. Return the pudding to the oven for 15-20 minutes, or until the meringue top has set. This is traditionally served cold.

—.—

## Dialect words and phrases from the Manchester area

**'A bally ann meal'** - a meal thrown together from whatever is available.

**'Bidding'** - an invitation to a funeral.

**'Boggart'** - a ghost or spirit, especially those which lived in holes.

**'Chitty'** - a young girl or lass, as in 'a chit of a girl'.

**'Claggy'** - sticky, can be used for to describe dough, mud or sticky weather.

**'Clough'** - a steep sided valley.

**'Delph'** - a quarry or excavation .

**'Fettle'** - to mend, or repair.

**'Hippins'** - babies' nappies.

**'Keks'** - trousers.

**'Mawkin'** - dirty or shabby.

**'Motty'** - a small amount of money.

**'Petty'** - an outdoor toilet.

**'Reasty' or 'resty'** - rotten, gone off (as of food).

**'Sennit'** - a week (seven nights).

**'Skrike'** - to cry out or shriek.

**'Spun up for bobbins'** - nothing to do.

**'Yammer'** - to want something badly.

Manchester, Market Street c1885  18266

# RECIPE

—·—

## Chester Pudding

There are two Chester Pudding recipes: the oldest is a steamed suet pudding with the addition of blackcurrant jam. The recipe given below is for the second, more recent, Chester Pudding, which is rather like a Bakewell Tart but with a meringue topping.

> 175g/6oz shortcrust pastry
> 115g/4oz caster sugar
> 50g/2oz butter
> 25g/1oz ground almonds
> 3 eggs, separated
> 1 tablespoonful caster sugar for the meringue
> Milk for glazing

Pre-heat oven to 190°C/375°F/Gas Mark 5.

Roll the pastry out very thinly, line a baking tin with it and brush the edges of the pastry with a little milk.

Carefully melt the sugar and butter in a heavy saucepan, and add the ground almonds. Allow the mixture to cool slightly, then stir in the three eggs yolks and one egg white. Gently cook the mixture over a low heat, stirring constantly, until it thickens, then pour it into the pastry-lined baking tin. Bake for 20 minutes. When the pastry and pudding filling is cooked, remove from the oven. Whisk the remaining two egg whites until stiff, then fold in the extra tablespoon of sugar. Spread the meringue mixture on top of the pudding. Reduce the heat of the oven to 170°C/325°F/Gas Mark 3, and bake the pudding for about 20 minutes, or until the meringue is firm and golden on the peaks. Serve hot or cold.

—·—

Manchester, No 9 Dock c1965  M21503

# RECIPE

—·—

## Jack Tart

175g/6oz shortcrust pastry
Raspberry jam
50g/2oz butter or margarine
50g/2oz caster sugar
115g/4oz rolled oats

Pre-heat the oven to 190°C/375°C/Gas Mark 5.

Roll out the pastry on a lightly floured surface and use it to line a greased ovenproof tart plate or pie tin. Spread the base of the pastry with a layer of the jam, leaving a jam-free border of about 1cm (half an inch) around the edge. Melt the butter or margarine with the sugar in a heavy-bottomed saucepan, and then stir in the oats and mix it all together well. Spread the mixture in an even layer on top of the jam. Crimp the pastry edge with your finger and thumb to make a decorative edge, and bake the tart in the pre-heated oven for about 30 minutes, until it is golden brown.

—·—

Lancaster, Queen Victoria Monument
1912 64217x

# TEATIME AND BAKING

Downham, The Village 1894  34357

# RECIPE

—·—

## Preston Gingerbread

350g/12oz plain flour

1 rounded teaspoonful ground ginger

A pinch of grated nutmeg

A pinch of mixed spice

50g/2oz softened butter

115g/4oz black treacle

Half a level teaspoonful of bicarbonate of soda

3 tablespoonfuls warm milk

1 beaten egg

Pre-heat the oven to 180°C/350°F/Gas Mark 4.

Grease and line a deep tin 25 x 20cm (10 x 8 inches). Sift the flour and spices into a mixing bowl, then rub in the butter until the mixture resembles fine breadcrumbs. Warm the treacle gently in a saucepan. Mix the bicarbonate of soda well into the warm milk, add to the treacle and pour into the flour mixture, combining thoroughly. Add the beaten egg and beat the mixture gently but thoroughly. Pour the mixture into the prepared tin and bake in the pre-heated oven for 45 minutes, or until firm when pressed. Leave to cool in the tin for 5 minutes before turning out on to a wire tray. This is best kept in an airtight tin for 2-3 days before eating.

—·—

# The Corn Laws

Three 19th-century men who were famous for their opposition to the hated Corn Laws, which banned the import of cheap foreign wheat and kept the price of bread high, are commemorated by statues in north-western towns. Manchester remembers Richard Cobden with a statue in St Ann's Square and his colleague John Bright, whose statue is in Albert Square. Rochdale also remembers John Bright, with a statue which now stands in Broadfield Park. In Bury, a statue of Sir Robert Peel, one of the area's most famous sons, stands in the Market Place; it was placed there in 1852 to commemorate his repeal of the Corn Laws in 1846 during his term as Prime Minister. Sir Robert Peel is also famous as the father of the modern police force in Britain; he set up the Metropolitan Police Force in London during his period of office as Home Secretary in the 1820s, giving rise to the nicknames of 'Peelers' or 'Bobbies' for policemen.

Manchester, St Ann's Square c1876  8290

Rochdale, John Bright's Statue 1898 41022

# RECIPE

—.—

## Bury Simnel Cakes

Bury Simnel Cakes were originally eaten on Mothering Sunday, but it later became traditional to serve them at Easter. The word 'simnel' probably derives from the Latin word 'simila', meaning 'fine', which may be a reference to the fine quality flour from which these cakes were made.

225g/8oz plain flour
Half a teaspoonful salt
Half a teaspoonful baking powder
Half a teaspoonful mixed spice
115g/4oz butter or margarine
75g/3oz chopped candied peel
150g/5oz currants
150g/5oz sultanas
75g/3oz chopped glace cherries
175g/6oz soft brown sugar
50g/2oz chopped blanched almonds
2 eggs

Pre-heat the oven to 190°C/375°F/Gas Mark 5.

Put the flour and butter into a large mixing bowl, and rub the butter or margarine into the flour. Add all the other ingredients except the eggs and almonds, and mix well. Add the eggs, and mix into a stiff dough, adding a little milk if the mix is too dry. Roll out the dough to about 1cm (half an inch) thick. Cut into small round cakes, and sprinkle with the chopped almonds. Bake on a greased baking tray in the pre-heated oven for about 45 minutes.

—.—

Bolton, Bradshawgate 1903 50157

# RECIPE

—·—

# North Country Parkin

Parkin is a dark sweet cake made from oatmeal instead of flour that is a heavy, sticky cake due to the liberal addition of black treacle. Parkin was traditionally eaten on Bonfire Night (or Guy Fawkes' Night) on 5th November, but its older tradition is associated with the feast days marking the beginning of winter, around the time of All Saints' (or All Hallows') Day on 1st November, and All Souls' Day on 2nd November. These Christian feast days themselves have origins in the ancient Celtic feast of the dead called Samhain. North Country Parkin came to be called 'Harcake' and would be offered to visitors on All Saints' Day, which commemorated the saints and martyrs of the Christian faith.

> 175g/6oz plain flour
> 1 teaspoonful salt
> 1 teaspoonful ground ginger
> 2 teaspoonfuls ground cinnamon
> 1 teaspoonful bicarbonate of soda
> 275g/10oz medium oatmeal
> 175g/6oz black treacle
> 150g/5oz butter
> 115g/4oz dark soft brown sugar
> 150ml/ ¼ pint milk
> 1 egg, beaten

Pre-heat the oven to 180°C/350°F/Gas Mark 4.

Sift together the flour, salt, spices and bicarbonate of soda. Add the oatmeal and mix it all well together. Warm the treacle, butter, sugar and milk together until the butter has melted. Cool slightly, then add the egg and beat well. Pour the treacle mixture into the centre of the dry ingredients and stir rapidly until smooth. Turn into a greased and lined 18-20cm (7-8 inch) square tin. Bake in the pre-heated oven for one hour. Store in an airtight tin, and keep for a few days – up to two weeks is best! – before eating. This can be eaten with a slice of Lancashire or Cheshire Cheese, depending on where your loyalties lie!

—·—

# Souling

November 1st, or All Souls' Eve, was the time when families remembered the souls of departed relatives, which were thought to return to their homes on this night – sometimes bonfires would be lit on the hills to light their way home. Prayers were said for the dead, and food was left on kitchen tables in the night. 'Souling' would also take place, when 'soulers' would travel from door to door begging for soul-cakes in return for songs and prayers. The traditional drink served to soulers (or 'cakers' as they sometimes known) was spiced ale. In some parts of the country this custom was spread over the three days of Halloween (31st October), All Saints' Day (1st November) and All Souls' Day (2nd November).

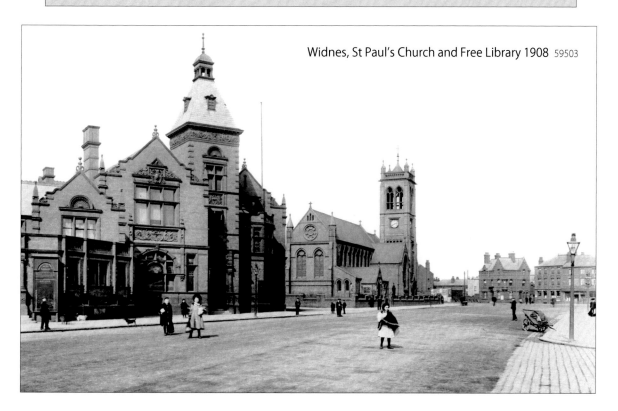

Widnes, St Paul's Church and Free Library 1908 59503

# RECIPE

~ . ~

## Oatcakes

In 'Glimpses of Macclesfield in Ye Olden Days' (1883) Isaac Finney makes the following comment: 'Another old custom we may not omit to notice, which was formerly practised in Macclesfield, previously noting that at that time oatcake, as an article of diet, was in more general use than now. On entering almost any house of the operatives, and indeed most of the upper classes of that time, you would have observed suspended from the ceiling of the kitchen a large open frame of wood, interlaced from all points with a network of cord, called an oatcake rack, on which were spread the week's supply of oatcakes, and which were reached down or pieces broken off as required for use, when a little treacle or butter was spread upon it and eaten, hard as it was, with a relish that few now-a-days would like to submit to'.

225g/8oz fine oatmeal
115g/4oz self-raising flour
A pinch of salt
Half a teaspoonful of bicarbonate of soda
50g/2oz butter or margarine
1 egg, beaten
Milk to mix

Pre-heat the oven to 180°C/350°F/Gas Mark 4.

Sieve the flour, salt and bicarbonate of soda together into a bowl. Rub in the fat until the mixture resembles fine breadcrumbs. Add the oatmeal, and mix it all together. Mix in the beaten egg and just enough milk to form a stiff dough. Turn out the dough onto a surface sprinkled with oatmeal and roll it out to about 5mm (¼ inch) thick, then rub the surface of the dough with more oatmeal. Cut the dough into large rounds with a pastry cutter and place the oatcakes on a greased baking sheet. Bake in the pre-heated oven for about 10 minutes. The oatcakes can be eaten with bacon and eggs etc, or spread with butter and served with cheese, or spread with honey, jam or golden syrup whilst still warm from the oven.

~ . ~

# 'Don't say brown – say Hovis.'

Macclesfield was the birthplace of Hovis bread, famous for the advertising slogan of 'Don't say brown, say Hovis'. Hovis bread is made from a special type of flour that is especially rich in wheatgerm, which was patented in 1899 by Richard Smith; the brand was developed by S Fitton & Sons Ltd, whose mill operated on the banks of the Macclesfield canal. The name 'Hovis' was invented by a London student, Herbert Grimes, who was inspired by the Latin phrase 'hominis vis' ('the strength of man'), after Fittons set a national competition to find a trading name for the bread made from their patented flour. Fittons milled the flour and sold it to bakers with specially branded baking tins. Fittons became Hovis Ltd in 1918, and after a succession of mergers became part of Rank Hovis McDougall in 1962. The company is now part of the food conglomerate RHM, but the Hovis side of the business still specialises in high wheatgerm wholemeal flour. The former Hovis warehouse by the canal is now a development of apartments.

# 'Treacle Town'

Although 'Silk Town' is the more usual nickname nowadays, Macclesfield's other nickname is 'Treacle Town'. Local tradition says that this derives from an incident when a merchant spilt a quantity of treacle on Hibel Road, which the local people were quick to salvage, although another explanation says that it dates from when some mill-owners in the town provided barrels of treacle to unemployed weavers.

# RECIPE

—·—

## Goosnargh Cakes

The north Lancashire village of Goosnargh is famous for Goosnargh Ducks and also for sweet, shortbready Goosnargh Cakes, which are flavoured with caraway seeds or coriander. They are made in the form of round biscuits, and were traditionally eaten at festivals and holidays, such as Easter and Whitsun. One Whitsuntide 50,000 cakes were sold at Goosnargh for the annual cake-eating feast.

> 200g/7oz plain flour
> 150g/5oz fresh unsalted butter
> 50g/2oz sugar
> 1 teaspoonful caraway seeds or ground coriander seeds

Pre-heat the oven to 180°C/350°F/Gas Mark 4.

Rub the butter into the flour, then stir in the sugar and the caraway or coriander seeds. Leave the mixture in a cool place for four hours for the flavour to infuse. Knead the mixture lightly, roll it out on a lightly floured surface and cut the dough into small rounds. Place the cakes on a greased baking tray and bake in the pre-heated oven for 15-20 minutes, until they are lightly golden – check during cooking to make sure they do not overcook. Sprinkle each cake with extra sugar to finish.

—·—

Altrincham, Tram in Stamford New Road
1907 58622x

# RECIPE

—·—

## Eccles Cakes

Eccles Cakes are made with flaky puff pastry gathered over a filling of dried fruit, sugar and spice. They have been linked with festivals, or 'wakes', in Eccles for centuries – it is said that the Puritans banned the eating of Eccles Cakes in the 17th century, as they were linked with the local celebrations when the people of the town danced on the green. Chorley Cakes are made in a similar way, but using shortcrust pastry. Sad Cakes, or 'Desolate Cakes', are another variation to Eccles Cakes that is found in the Rossendale area.

>  450g/1 lb flaky or puff pastry
>  175g/6oz currants
>  25g/1oz butter, softened at room temperature
>  50g/2oz soft brown sugar
>  25g/1oz chopped mixed peel
>  Pinch of ground nutmeg
>  1 egg white, lightly beaten
>  Caster sugar, to finish

Pre-heat the oven to 220°C/425°F/Gas Mark 7.

Roll out the pastry thinly on a lightly floured surface, and cut it into 10cm (4 inch) rounds. Mix the currants, butter, sugar, peel and nutmeg well together, and put a heaped teaspoonful of the mixture on to each pastry round. Dampen the edges of each round, gather them together in the centre and pinch the edges to seal. Turn the rounds over, and roll them out very gently until they are a circular shape and the fruit just begins to show through the pastry. Put the cakes on to a greased baking sheet and score the top of each cake twice with a sharp knife, to form two slashes across the surface. Brush each cake lightly with the beaten egg white and sprinkle with caster sugar. Bake in the pre-heated oven for about 20 minutes, until the pastry is golden brown.

—·—

# 'The Breadbasket of Lancashire'

It was the drainage of acres of swamp and bog that truly brought The Fylde area of Lancashire into its own: these areas include Pilling, Stalmine, Rawliffe, Thornton, Hambleton, Nateby and Winmarleigh. Drained for agriculture, and with some areas where peat was cut for valuable fuel, these mosslands became productive, and were known as 'the golden cornfield of Amounderness' and The Fylde became 'the breadbasket of Lancashire'.

As time went on and more statuesque tower mills to grind corn replaced the old wooden peg mills, 'Windmill Land' became an apt description for the area. Marsh Mill at Thornton Cleveleys, built by Bold Fleetwood Hesketh, is now the only working windmill in the Fylde. In the 1950s repair work was done, and in 1979 a new oak beam on which the sails rested was hoisted into place. Marsh Mill has been painted white, and its brilliant red sails spin round while visitors view the interior.

Thornton Cleveleys, Marsh Mill c1955 T307001

# RECIPE

— · —

## Sally Cake

Sally Cake is particularly appropriate to Rochdale, where the famous singer Gracie Fields, 'The Lassie from Lancashire', was born in 1898. 'Sally from our Alley' was one of her most famous songs.

> 115g/4oz brown sugar
> 115g/4oz raisins
> 50g/2oz butter
> 225g/8oz plain flour
> 5 level teaspoonfuls baking powder
> 250ml/8 fl oz water
> 1 teaspoonful ground nutmeg
> 1 teaspoonful ground cinnamon
> Half a teaspoonful salt

Pre-heat the oven to 160°C/325°F/Gas Mark 3.

Put the butter, raisins, sugar, spices and water into a large saucepan. Bring to the boil, and continue boiling for 2 minutes, stirring occasionally, then remove the pan from the heat and allow the mixture to cool slightly. Sieve the flour, salt and baking powder together and gently fold it into the mixture to form a soft dropping consistency. Pour the mixture into a greased and lined cake tin. Bake in the pre-heated oven for about one hour, until the cake is well risen and golden brown.

— · —

Rochdale, Church Steps 1913 65603

# RECIPE

## Chester Buns

115g/4oz butter or margarine
900g/2 lbs plain flour
50g/2oz caster sugar
Pinch of salt
1 egg
300ml/10 fl oz condensed milk
15g/½ oz fresh yeast, or 1½ teaspoonfuls quick-acting dried yeast

Dissolve the yeast in 150ml/5 fl oz of warm water, add one teaspoonful of the sugar, then leave it until it becomes frothy. Rub the fat into the flour and stir in the rest of the sugar and the salt. Warm the condensed milk in a saucepan, remove from heat and beat the egg into it. Add the prepared yeast mixture, mix it all into a dough and then cover the dough and leave it in a warm place for about one hour, until it has risen and doubled in size. Knead the dough lightly again, then form it into buns and place them on a greased baking sheet. Cover and leave the buns in a warm place again to rise once more.

Pre-heat the oven to 200°C/400°F/Gas Mark 6. When the buns have risen, place the baking sheet in the pre-heated oven and bake for about 20 minutes. When cooked, brush the buns with a sugar and water wash whilst they are still warm, to glaze.

# RECIPE

—·—

## Chester Cake

Chester Cake is a good way of using up left-over pieces of stale cake. It is made with black treacle or golden syrup, currants and ginger, and cut into small squares after baking.

225g/8oz shortcrust pastry
115g/4oz plain flour
15g/ ½ oz baking powder
225g/8oz stale cake pieces, crumbled
175g/6oz black treacle or golden syrup, whichever is preferred
25g/1oz currants
A pinch of ground ginger
1 egg, beaten
2 tablespoonfuls of milk

Pre-heat the oven to 200°C/400°C/Gas Mark 6.

Line the bottom and sides of a greased deep cake tin or Yorkshire pudding tin with the pastry, reserving enough pastry to make a lid. Sieve the flour and baking powder together into a basin. Add the cake crumbs, currants and ginger, treacle or golden syrup, and combine it all together to form a stiff mixture. Spread the mixture over the base of the pastry in the tin. Roll out the reserved pastry to form a lid and place it over the mixture, pinching the pastry edges together to seal them. Brush the lid with the beaten egg mixed with the milk, and mark the surface into small squares. Bake the cake in the pre-heated oven for about 20 minutes. When cold, divide it into squares with a sharp knife along the lines marked on the pastry before baking.

—·—

# RECITE

~·~

## Tosset Cakes

Tosset Cakes were once the customary fare to be eaten at funerals in Lancashire.

> 225g/8oz plain flour
> 115g/4oz butter or margarine
> 25g/1oz caster sugar
> Half a teaspoonful ground cinnamon

Pre-heat the oven to 200°C/400°F/Gas Mark 6.

Cream the butter and sugar together until the mixture is light and fluffy. Sieve the flour and cinnamon together, fold into the mixture and mix it all to form a smooth dough. Roll the dough out on a lightly floured surface until it is quite thin, and cut it into small rounds using a pastry cutter. Place the rounds on a greased baking sheet in bake in the pre-heated oven for 20 minutes, or until the cakes are golden brown.

~·~

Warrington, The Knutsford Road Swing Bridge c1960  W29056

Northwich, Crossing the Swing Bridge 1900  45422x

# RECIPE

—.—

## Fig Pie

Fig Pie was traditionally served in Lancashire on Mothering Sunday.

> 175g/6oz shortcrust pastry
> 225g/8oz figs, fresh or dried (see cooking instructions below)
> 1 level dessertspoonful of cornflour
> Half a teaspoonful of ground mixed spice
> 25g/1oz currants
> 1 dessertspoonful of black treacle or golden syrup, whichever is preferred

Roll out the pastry on a lightly floured surface and use it to line a greased deep pie tin or dish. Cut the stalks off the figs and place the fruit in a shallow saucepan with just enough water to cover them; cook over a low heat until the figs are tender. (Fresh figs need about 5-15 minutes, depending on their ripeness; dried figs should first be soaked for 12 hours with a squeeze of lemon juice before being stewed for 20 minutes in their soaking liquid.)

Pre-heat the oven to 200°C/400°C/Gas Mark 6.

Drain the figs and retain 300ml/ ½ pint of the liquid – top up to this amount with hot water if necessary. Pour a little of the juice into a basin, add the cornflour and mix until it resembles a thin smooth cream. Gradually add the rest of the liquid, stirring well. When well mixed, return it to the saucepan and place over moderate heat. Stir until thickened, then cook for a further 2 minutes. Mix in the spice, currants and treacle or syrup and remove from the heat.

Arrange the figs over the pastry in the pie tin or dish. Pour over the thickened fig liquid, making sure that the currants are evenly distributed. Bake on the middle shelf of the pre-heated oven for 30-35 minutes. Can be eaten hot or cold.

—.—

Bowdon, The Polygon, Stamford Road 1907  58602

New Brighton, The Pier 1900 45166

# INDEX OF PHOTOGRAPHS

Accrington, Blackburn Road 1899 43496 — 34
Altrincham, Old Houses 1903 49669x — 53
Altrincham A Tram in Stamford New Road 1907 58622x — 73
Blackburn, The Market and Town Hall 1894 34307 — 24
Blackpool, Imperial Hydropathic Establishment 1890 22890 — 48
Blackpool, From North Pier 1906 53853 — 8
Blackpool, North Shore 1890 22886 — 5
Blackpool, The South Jetty from the Wellington Hotel 1890 22881 — 10-11
Bolton, Bradshawgate 1903 50157 — 67
Bowdon, The Polygon, Stamford Road 1907 58602 — 83
Bury, Market Place 1895 36782 — 33
Bury, The Market 1902 48562 — 32
Chester, The Cross 1903 49881 — 42
Chester, Eastgate Street 1923 73865 — 18
Clitheroe, Friends 1894 34346x — Title page
Congleton, Lawton Street 1898 42154 — 51
Downham, The Village 1894 34357 — 62
Fleetwood, The Barrow Boat 1908 59940 — 12
Fleetwood, The Harbour 1894 33968 — 17
Lancaster, Queen Victoria Monument 1912 64217x — 61
Lancaster, The Town Hall 1886 18091 — 39
Liverpool, Dale Street 1887 20002 — 27
Liverpool, The London and North Western Railway Hotel 1890 26662 — 28
Lymm, The Bridgewater Canal c1960 L122054 — 88
Lytham, The Pier and Donkeys 1914 67480 — 7
Macclesfield, Chestergate 1898 42600x — 44-45
Manchester, St Ann's Square c1876 8290 — 64
Manchester, Market Street c1885 18266 — 56-57
Manchester, No 9 Dock c1965 M21503 — 59
Morecambe, Entrance, The Central Pier 1888 21080x — 12
Nether Alderley, Village Smithy 1896 37477a — 26
New Brighton, The Pier 1900 45166 — 84-85
New Brighton, Tower and Sands 1900 45163 — 20
Northwich, Crossing the Swing Bridge 1900 45422x — 81
Ormskirk, Church Street 1894 34138 — 30
Parkgate, Loading Mussels 1939 P255011 — 20
Preston, Church Street 1903 50069 — 6
Preston, Moor Park Avenue 1903 50088 — 36
Rochdale, Church Steps 1913 65603 — 77
Rochdale, John Bright's Statue 1898 41022 — 65
Runcorn, The Locks c1955 R67003 — 40
Southport, Lord Street 1913 66508 — 48
Southport, The Sands 1902 48588 — 14
St Anne's, The Sands 1914 67490 — 22-23
Styal, The Cotton Mill 1897 39616 — 37
Thornton Cleveleys, Marsh Mill c1955 T307001 — 75
Wallasey, May Cottage and the Nook 1898 W164012 — 47
Warrington, Church Street 1894 33805 — 41
Warrington, The Knutsford Road Swing Bridge c1960 W29056 — 81
Widnes, St Paul's Church and Free Library 1908 59503 — 69

# INDEX OF RECIPES

| | |
|---|---|
| Beefsteak Pie with Lancashire Cheese Crust | 31 |
| Bury Simnel Cakes | 66 |
| Cheshire Cheese Soup | 41 |
| Cheshire Fidget Pie | 25 |
| Cheshire Onion Pie | 43 |
| Chester Buns | 78 |
| Chester Cake | 79 |
| Chester Potted Cheese | 42 |
| Chester Pudding | 58 |
| Damson and Apple Tansy | 52 |
| Eccles Cakes | 74 |
| Fig Pie | 82 |
| Gooseberry and Elderflower Cream | 50 |
| Goosnargh Cakes | 72 |
| Jack Tart | 60 |
| Herrings with Mustard Sauce | 16-17 |
| Hindle Wakes | 38 |
| Lancashire Hotpot | 35 |
| Mackerel, Stuffed, with Gooseberry Sauce | 15 |
| Manchester Pudding | 54 |
| Mussels with Parsley | 21 |
| North Country Parkin | 68 |
| Oatcakes | 70 |
| Parched Peas | 7 |
| Pease Pudding | 9 |
| Potato and Onion Cakes | 46 |
| Potted Shrimps | 13 |
| Preston Gingerbread | 63 |
| Sally Cake | 76 |
| Salmon Baked in Pastry | 19 |
| Scouse | 29 |
| Summer Pudding | 49 |
| Tosset Cakes | 80 |

Lymm, The Bridgewater Canal c1960 L122054

# FRITH PRODUCTS & SERVICES

Francis Frith would doubtless be pleased to know that the pioneering publishing venture he started in 1860 still continues today. Over a hundred and forty years later, The Francis Frith Collection continues in the same innovative tradition and is now one of the foremost publishers of vintage photographs in the world. Some of the current activities include:

## INTERIOR DECORATION

Today Frith's photographs can be seen framed and as giant wall murals in thousands of pubs, restaurants, hotels, banks, retail stores and other public buildings throughout the country. In every case they enhance the unique local atmosphere of the places they depict and provide reminders of gentler days in an increasingly busy and frenetic world.

## PRODUCT PROMOTIONS

Frith products are used by many major companies to promote the sales of their own products or to reinforce their own history and heritage. Frith promotions have been used by Hovis bread, Courage beers, Scots Porage Oats, Colman's mustard, Cadbury's foods, Mellow Birds coffee, Dunhill pipe tobacco, Guinness, and Bulmer's Cider.

## GENEALOGY AND FAMILY HISTORY

As the interest in family history and roots grows world-wide, more and more people are turning to Frith's photographs of Great Britain for images of the towns, villages and streets where their ancestors lived; and, of course, photographs of the churches and chapels where their ancestors were christened, married and buried are an essential part of every genealogy tree and family album.

## FRITH PRODUCTS

All Frith photographs are available Framed or just as Mounted Prints and Posters (size 23 x 16 inches). These may be ordered from the address below. Other products available are- Address Books, Calendars, Jigsaws, Canvas Prints, Notelets and local and prestige books.

## THE INTERNET

Already ninety thousand Frith photographs can be viewed and purchased on the internet through the Frith websites and a myriad of partner sites.

For more detailed information on Frith companies and products, look at this site:
www.francisfrith.com

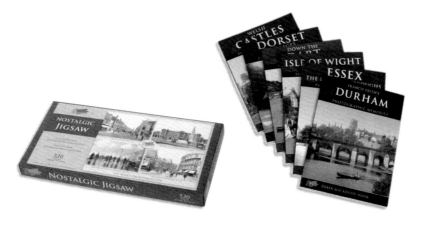

**See the complete list of Frith Books at: www.francisfrith.com**
This web site is regularly updated with the latest list of publications from The Francis Frith Collection. If you wish to buy books relating to another part of the country that your local bookshop does not stock, you may purchase on-line.

*For further information, trade, or author enquiries please contact us at the address below:*
**The Francis Frith Collection, Unit 6, Oakley Business Park, Wylye Road, Dinton, Wiltshire SP3 5EU.**
Tel: +44 (0)1722 716 376  Fax: +44 (0)1722 716 881   Email: sales@francisfrith.co.uk

See Frith products on the internet at www.francisfrith.com

# FREE PRINT OF YOUR CHOICE

### Mounted Print
*Overall size 14 x 11 inches (355 x 280mm)*

**Choose any Frith photograph in this book.**
Simply complete the Voucher opposite and return it with your remittance for £3.50 (to cover postage and handling) and we will print the photograph of your choice in SEPIA (size 11 x 8 inches) and supply it in a cream mount with a burgundy rule line (overall size 14 x 11 inches).
**Please note: aerial photographs and photographs with a reference number starting with a "Z" are not Frith photographs and cannot be supplied under this offer. Offer valid for delivery to one UK address only.**

*PLUS:* **Order additional Mounted Prints at HALF PRICE - £10.00 each** (normally £20.00)
If you would like to order more Frith prints from this book, possibly as gifts for friends and family, you can buy them at half price (with no additional postage and handling costs).

*PLUS:* **Have your Mounted Prints framed**
For an extra £19.00 per print you can have your mounted print(s) framed in an elegant polished wood and gilt moulding, overall size 16 x 13 inches (no additional postage and handling required).

---

### IMPORTANT!

**These special prices are only available if you use this form to order. You must use the ORIGINAL VOUCHER on this page (no copies permitted). We can only despatch to one UK address. This offer cannot be combined with any other offer.**

---

*Send completed Voucher form to:*
**The Francis Frith Collection, Unit 6, Oakley Business Park, Wylye Road, Dinton, Wiltshire SP3 5EU**

# CHOOSE A PHOTOGRAPH FROM THIS BOOK

*Voucher* for **FREE** and Reduced Price Frith Prints

*Please do not photocopy this voucher. Only the original is valid, so please fill it in, cut it out and return it to us with your order.*

| Picture ref no | Page no | Qty | Mounted @ £10.00 | Framed + £19.00 | Total Cost £ |
|---|---|---|---|---|---|
| | | 1 | Free of charge* | £ | £ |
| | | | £10.00 | £ | £ |
| | | | £10.00 | £ | £ |
| | | | £10.00 | £ | £ |
| | | | £10.00 | £ | £ |
| | | | £10.00 | £ | £ |

*Please allow 28 days for delivery. Offer available to one UK address only*

| | | |
|---|---|---|
| * Post & handling | | £3.50 |
| **Total Order Cost** | | £ |

Title of this book . . . . . . . . . . . . . . . . . . . . . . . . . . . . .
I enclose a cheque/postal order for £ . . . . . . . . . . .
made payable to 'The Francis Frith Collection'

OR please debit my Mastercard / Visa / Maestro card, details below

Card Number:

Issue No (Maestro only):          Valid from (Maestro):

Card Security Number:              Expires:

Signature:

Name  Mr/Mrs/Ms .................................................
Address ............................................................
.........................................................................
.........................................................................
.................................... Postcode .......................
Daytime Tel No ....................................................
Email ................................................................

Valid to 31/12/14

**Free Print – see overleaf**

### Can you help us with information about any of the Frith photographs in this book?

We are gradually compiling an historical record for each of the photographs in the Frith archive. It is always fascinating to find out the names of the people shown in the pictures, as well as insights into the shops, buildings and other features depicted.

If you recognize anyone in the photographs in this book, or if you have information not already included in the author's caption, do let us know. We would love to hear from you, and will try to publish it in future books or articles.

### An Invitation from The Francis Frith Collection to Share Your Memories

The 'Share Your Memories' feature of our website allows members of the public to add personal memories relating to the places featured in our photographs, or comment on others already added. Seeing a place from your past can rekindle forgotten or long held memories. Why not visit the website, find photographs of places you know well and add YOUR story for others to read and enjoy? We would love to hear from you!

**www.francisfrith.com/memories**

### Our production team

Frith books are produced by a small dedicated team at offices near Salisbury. Most have worked with the Frith Collection for many years. All have in common one quality: they have a passion for the Frith Collection.

### Frith Books and Gifts

We have a wide range of books and gifts available on our website utilising our photographic archive, many of which can be individually personalised.

**www.francisfrith.com**

FF004083